Cornerstones of Freedom

The Manhattan Project

R. Conrad Stein

CHILDRENS PRESS®

CHICAGO

Library of Congress Cataloging-in-Publication Data

Stein, R. Conrad.
  The Manhattan Project / by R. Conrad Stein.
    p. cm. — (Cornerstones of freedom)
  Summary: Recounts the history of the crash program
that resulted in the development of the atomic bomb.
  ISBN 0-516-06670-6
  1. Manhattan Project (U.S.)—History—Juvenile
literature. 2. Atomic bomb—United States—History—
Juvenile literature. [1. Manhattan Project
(U.S.) 2. Atomic bomb.] I. Title. II. Series.
QC773.3.U5S84 1993
355.8'25119'09—dc20   93-12686
                                                          CIP
                                                           AC

July 16, 1945. The New Mexico desert near the town of Alamogordo.

In a concrete bunker, a group of scientists and high-ranking military officials waited tensely. Many of them glanced at the clock, which ticked toward five in the morning. It was still too dark to see the hundred-foot-tall steel tower that rose out of the desert sands some ten thousand yards in front of the bunker. Resting on the top of that tower was the world's first atomic bomb.

The scientists hoped—and some of them feared—that this test bomb, nicknamed "Fat Man," would produce a unique explosion. A nuclear explosion sets tiny atomic particles shattering into fragments. The fragments in turn shatter other particles, causing the release of a tremendous amount of energy. This is called a nuclear chain reaction. If the test worked, the U.S. government might use such a bomb to help bring World War II to an end.

"Zero minus ten seconds," said a voice over the bunker's loudspeaker. Now all eyes gazed at the clock. It was history's first countdown: "four . . . three . . . two . . . one. . . ."

"Suddenly there was an enormous flash of light," wrote scientist Isidor Rabi. "[It was] the

The tower that held the world's first atomic bomb

Isidor Rabi

brightest light I have ever seen or that I think anyone has ever seen. It blasted; it pounced; it bored its way right through you. It was a vision which was seen with more than the eye. It was seen to last forever. You wished it would stop. . . . There was an enormous ball of fire which grew and grew and it rolled as it grew; it went up in the air in yellow flashes and into scarlet and green. It looked menacing. It seemed to come toward me."

Finally, the tremendous ball of fire reached its zenith and diminished. The dim morning sunlight revealed a mushroom-shaped cloud rising from the desert floor.

The world's first atomic bomb was tested on July 16, 1945, near Alamogordo, New Mexico. "Trinity" was the code name for the test.

SHOCK FRONT

BALL OF FIRE

MACH FRONT

DIRT CLOUD

The mushroom cloud climbed 42,000 feet into the New Mexico sky.

In the bunker, the men displayed mixed reactions. Some congratulated each other with slaps on the back, because the weapon they had worked so long to build was now a proven success. Others simply sat in stunned silence, fearing they had created a monster. General Leslie Groves, the military commander of the atomic-bomb development project, turned to his aide and said, "The war is over. One or two of those things and Japan will be finished." Robert Oppenheimer, the chief scientist, was more solemn. He recalled a passage from the *Bhagavad-Gita*, an ancient book of Hindu religious scripture: "Now I am become Death, the destroyer of worlds."

Robert Oppenheimer

Two months after the Trinity test, Robert Oppenheimer and General Leslie Groves viewed what was left of the tower that had held the world's first atomic device.

The success of the test meant that the United States had created the most powerful weapon ever devised by humankind. The bomb's destructive power stunned even its creators. The scientists had hoped their invention would explode with the force of a thousand tons of TNT. The test device turned out to be twenty times that powerful. The steel tower that supported the bomb vanished without a trace. Beneath the blast, the desert sand was fused into a half-mile ring of glass. All plants and animals in the vicinity, including rattlesnakes and cacti, were killed. Four hundred years earlier, Spanish explorers traveling over this waterless region had given it a name that was now eerily appropriate. The Spaniards called it *Jornada del Muerto*— Journey of Death.

The atomic bomb was built by a top-secret government program called the Manhattan Project. The men and women employed by the Manhattan Project started their work in the early 1940s, just after America entered World War II. But long before the war, scientists had pondered the amazing and complex world of the atom.

All matter is made up of atoms. So tiny are these particles that they could not be seen by even the most powerful microscopes available in the 1940s. Still, scientists at the time knew about the structure of individual atoms. Every atom has a central core called a nucleus. The nucleus is made up of particles called protons and neutrons. Orbiting around the nucleus are one or more much smaller particles, called electrons.

In the 1930s, some scientists theorized that bombarding an atom's nucleus with a neutron from another atom would cause the first atom to split in two. The splitting atom would release another neutron, which would then strike a neighboring atom, causing it to split, and so on. It was thought that each splitting atom would release a tiny spark of energy. In a nuclear chain reaction, trillions upon trillions of atoms would split in less than a millionth of a second, thereby giving forth an awesome burst of power. This process of deriving energy through a chain reaction is called nuclear fission.

One of the leading scientists interested in nuclear fission was Leo Szilard, who was born in Hungary and educated at German universities. He was a gifted physicist whose brother once remarked, "Leo looked like an atomic scientist even when he was one year old." One day, while visiting London in 1933, Szilard waited for a green light so he could cross the street. Being a devoted scientist, he thought about atomic structure as he waited. When the light turned green, a question flashed into his mind: What if he could find an element that would emit two neutrons each time it was bombarded by one neutron? He later wrote, "Such an element could surely sustain a nuclear chain reaction."

Adolf Hitler

While Szilard worked to advance his idea, Adolf Hitler and the Nazi party took over Germany. Under Hitler's rule, Germany began building tanks, military airplanes, and bombs. At the time, German scientists led the world in nuclear physics. Szilard feared that Nazi Germany could develop an atomic bomb and become powerful enough to rule the world.

Sensing that war would soon break out in Europe, Szilard moved to the United States in

Leo Szilard (left) and Edward Teller (right)

1938. Shortly after he moved, German scientists shocked the scientific world by announcing that they had split uranium atoms by bombarding them with neutrons. For the first time in history, the atom had been smashed through man-made means. The next year, Austrian scientists showed that this splitting process was indeed acccompanied by a tremendous release of energy. Germany was now years ahead of rival nations in developing nuclear fission.

On a muggy day in July 1939, Szilard left his New York City apartment and drove east. With him in the car was Edward Teller, another Hungarian-born physicist who had studied in Germany. The two men drove to the Long Island home of Albert Einstein. Einstein was such a famous scientist that he could get the attention of powerful government leaders, including

President Franklin D. Roosevelt. Over cups of tea, Szilard and Teller told Einstein that they believed Germany would soon be able to make an atomic bomb. They asked Einstein to alert American authorities to this danger. Einstein, a gentle genius, had long dreamed of the possibility of using nuclear fission for positive purposes, such as fueling generator plants to provide abundant electricity. Only during his meeting with Szilard and Teller did he come to the shocking realization that atomic energy could also be used to make a bomb of hideous destructive force.

Einstein immediately wrote a letter to President Roosevelt that read, in part, "I believe, therefore, that it is my duty to bring to your attention [that] . . . it may become possible to set

In 1939, Albert Einstein (left) wrote a letter warning President Roosevelt (right) that Germany was capable of building an atomic bomb.

World War II began in September 1939, when Hitler's forces invaded Poland.

up a nuclear chain reaction in a large mass of uranium by which vast amounts of power and large quantities of new radium-like elements would be generated. A single bomb of this type, carried by boat and exploded in a port, might very well destroy the whole port, together with some of the surrounding territory."

Two whole months passed before Einstein's letter reached the president. Roosevelt was preoccupied with frightening events taking place in Europe. In September 1939, Germany invaded neighboring Poland. Moving with electrifying speed, German tanks and infantry struck deep into Poland's heartland. World War II had begun.

Roosevelt finally read Einstein's letter in October 1939. He ordered a committee of scientists and military officers to meet with

Szilard and Teller to determine whether America was capable of building a nuclear bomb. Generals and admirals attending the meeting scoffed at the idea of creating such a superweapon. To the military men, the bomb seemed like an idea dreamed up by a science-fiction writer.

Nevertheless, Szilard and Teller were granted a small amount of money and allowed to begin experiments in nuclear fission. The two scientists enlisted the aid of Italian-born physicist Enrico Fermi. Fermi had won the 1938 Nobel Prize in Physics for his work in nuclear research.

An atom smasher at Notre Dame's nuclear research laboratory in 1941

Enrico Fermi headed the project to create the first controlled, self-sustaining nuclear chain reaction.

Since much of America's early nuclear research had been conducted at New York's Columbia University, the federal government assigned the Manhattan District of the Army Corps of Engineers to construct the initial research and production facilities for the project. Hence, the "Manhattan Project" became the code name for the atomic-bomb development program. But the project also encompassed research work being carried out at the University of California at Berkeley and the University of Chicago.

Fermi and his assistants built the world's first nuclear reactor in a squash court beneath this football stadium at the University of Chicago.

In early 1942, the Manhattan Project moved its headquarters to Chicago. There the scientists set up a laboratory under the stands of a stadium once used by the University of Chicago's football team. The University of Chicago was an intellectual giant among the nation's colleges, but its student body showed little interest in football. Consequently, a laboratory under the bleachers was a quiet, isolated place to work.

In Chicago, the top scientists worked together, but they also had bitter arguments. Fermi believed in a cautious, step-by-step approach to achieving nuclear fission. Szilard, who was inspired by visions like the one he had on the London street corner, preferred to act on bursts of creative insight. Teller was the sternest of the three; he viewed American development of the bomb as almost a holy mission.

Despite their bickering, the Manhattan Project scientists assembled on December 2, 1942, to attempt the world's first controlled nuclear chain reaction. In a squash court beneath the football stands, technicians had built a nuclear reactor the size of a house. The outside of the structure consisted of forty-five thousand graphite bricks. Graphite, the material that goes into ordinary pencil lead, has the property to deflect speeding neutrons. Inside the reactor were nineteen thousand balls of uranium. The reaction was to be controlled by neutron-absorbing rods that were inserted in holes in the huge graphite house.

Enrico Fermi was in charge of this vitally important and potentially dangerous test. With a nod, Fermi ordered a technician to slowly pull

Some of the graphite bricks used to build the nuclear reactor at the University of Chicago

Scientists observing the first controlled nuclear chain reaction

out one of the rods, thereby allowing the reaction to begin. Clicking noises came from a special machine that counted neutron bombardments. As the technician pulled the rod out farther, the clicking sound was like popcorn bursting and striking the cover of a pan. The rod was inched out still farther. The clicking became a loud buzz. The meter on the counting machine jumped to the highest point of the scale and pinned itself there. "Gentlemen, the pile has gone critical," Fermi announced, meaning that history's first controlled nuclear chain reaction had indeed taken place. Fermi then ordered the control rod to be pushed back before the reactor blew up, perhaps taking a large part of Chicago with it.

The chain reaction achieved under the Unversity of Chicago football stands proved that a nuclear bomb could be made. Most of the scientists were overjoyed. But Szilard said to Fermi, "This is a black day for mankind."

The success at Chicago prompted President Roosevelt to give top priority to the creation of an atomic bomb. The focus of the Manhattan Project would now shift from bomb research to actual bomb production. No amount of money would be spared. More than $2 billion was finally spent on the effort. The Manhattan Project team would be allowed to employ the country's brightest mathematicians and its most highly trained technical people. Twelve Nobel prizewinners were enlisted in the undertaking. Highly skilled men and women were in short supply in wartime America, but they were routinely snatched off other jobs and set to work building the bomb.

Roosevelt believed he was in a race with Hitler to develop this ultimate weapon. In the early 1940s, rumors had leaked into Washington that Germany was building its own nuclear bomb. The Germans had taken over a heavy-water plant in Norway. Heavy water—water that contains an isotope called deuterium—is a crucial ingredient in making an atomic bomb. American spies reported that the Germans were mining uranium in occupied Czechoslovakia. All this evidence added up to a nightmare scenario. No one wanted to imagine what might happen if an atomic bomb fell into the hands of a madman such as Hitler.

The Manhattan Project was the most ambitious scientific undertaking ever launched in American history. Rare uranium had to be processed. Giant machinery needed for the bomb's development was designed and built on a piece-by-piece basis, like components in a precise clock. Work on the project was conducted in thirty-seven installations spread over thirteen different states. Two new towns—Hanford, Washington; and Oak Ridge, Tennessee—were created just to produce the material that would

Oak Ridge, Tennessee, was created to produce the bomb fuel U-235.

Weekly meetings allowed an exchange of ideas among the Manhattan Project scientists.

fuel the bomb. By 1945, Oak Ridge had been transformed from an isolated valley holding a few farms into the fifth-largest city in Tennessee.

The actual design and construction of the atomic bomb was carried out at another new town: Los Alamos, New Mexico. Before the war, Los Alamos had been a tiny ranch used as a boys' school. With breathtaking speed, houses and buildings were erected at Los Alamos. Soon the town had its own newspaper, schools, and a population of four thousand. Most Los Alamos residents were scientists and their families. The head of the Los Alamos project was the brilliant but brooding J. Robert Oppenheimer.

Physics professor Robert Oppenheimer (right) directed the Los Alamos laboratory that developed and built the actual bomb.

Oppenheimer had been born in 1904 to a wealthy family in New York City. As a boy, he awed his teachers with his genius in mathematics and physics. Despite his powerful intellect, Oppenheimer was gripped by dark moods and suicidal thoughts. But problems in complex science challenged his mind and made him as happy as he ever became. He became a physics professor, and in the 1930s, turned the University of California at Berkeley into the nation's top school of theoretical physics. In 1942, after having worked on important nuclear research at Berkeley for some time, he was named to direct Project Y, the group that would design the actual bomb.

It was Oppenheimer who suggested Los Alamos as the site for the design laboratory. As a child, he had spent summer vacations in the area, and had fond memories of exploring the region while pursuing his favorite youthful hobby—rock hunting.

Leslie Groves

The overall military command of the Manhattan Project was given to General Leslie Groves. Keeping the project's work a secret was an obsession with him. A small army of security guards stood vigil over all the plants and laboratories. Although more than a hundred thousand men and women took part in the effort, only a handful knew they were making an atomic bomb. Those few who did know the goal of the Manhattan Project were careful to call the bomb a "gadget" or a "gizmo" in casual conversation. In

Because the bomb-building project had to be kept top secret, security at Los Alamos was extremely tight. Residents had to pass through two guard stations (left), and mounted guards patrolled the area (right).

The work at Los Alamos resulted in "Fat Man," the world's first atomic bomb (shown here being raised to the top of the tower).

Groves's mind, spies lurked everywhere, and not all of them were German. Many of the undertaking's top scientists were Jews who had been driven out of Europe by Nazi persecution. Surely it was unlikely that Jewish refugees would secretly work for the Germans. But Groves and other army leaders feared communist Russia would become a postwar enemy. The theory of communism appealed to many intellectuals in the 1920s and 1930s. Some of the Manhattan Project's scientists had embraced communist beliefs when they were young. Groves, a suspicious man by nature, employed his own detective force to check on the activities of scientists whose loyalty he questioned.

The war in Europe took a dramatic turn in June 1944, when Allied armies stormed the beaches in France and began a long march toward Germany. Traveling with the frontline forces was a top-secret unit code-named ALSOS. The ALSOS team investigated research sites in Europe where American scientists believed Germans were making a nuclear bomb. The ALSOS investigation discovered shocking evidence that Germany was not actively working to develop a nuclear bomb at all. Early in the war, the German military had shown interest in nuclear weapons, but it later shifted its scientific resources into making rockets and jet aircraft. Hitler himself led the country away from atomic-

Soon after the invasion of Normandy (left), an Allied intelligence unit learned that Germany had not, in fact, been building a nuclear bomb.

Rather than building an atomic bomb, Germany had put its energy into developing rockets and jet aircraft (right), shown here in a hidden, underground factory.

weapon development by denouncing nuclear physics as a "Jewish science."

Germany surrendered to the Allies on May 8, 1945. A week earlier, Hitler had committed suicide in a Berlin bunker. With the war in Europe over, Japan stood as America's only enemy.

In 1945, Japan was a nation near defeat. Her once-mighty navy lay at the bottom of the Pacific. Her air force was almost nonexistent. Huge American B-29 bombers soared through Japanese skies, pounding cities at will. Many Manhattan Project scientists declared it would be inhumane to drop the atomic bomb on such a helpless nation. Leo Szilard was the loudest protester. Szilard wrote a letter to the American president, begging him not to use on Japan the terrible weapon Szilard had helped create.

Harry Truman

In the White House was President Harry S. Truman. He had taken over as the nation's leader after Roosevelt died suddenly on April 12, 1945. Truman rejected Szilard's pleas. He pointed out that Japan's desperation had caused her soldiers to fight with fanatical courage. Okinawa, the last great Pacific island battle, had cost the Americans fifty thousand men killed or wounded. Military experts estimated that an invasion of the main Japanese islands could result in a million American casualties. Dropping the bomb would most likely force Japanese surrender and thereby prevent such an invasion.

The ground crew of the Enola Gay, the plane that dropped the atomic bomb on Hiroshima, Japan

Before dawn on August 6, 1945, a single B-29 named *Enola Gay* rumbled into the air from a runway at Tinian Island, about fifteen hundred miles south of Japan. The bomber was loaded with one whale-shaped bomb that weighed about nine thousand pounds. This solitary bomb, though nicknamed "Little Boy," packed more explosive power than could be carried by a thousand B-29s armed with conventional weapons.

Far ahead of the *Enola Gay*, a scout plane radioed that there was little cloud cover over the primary target—the Japanese city of Hiroshima. It was eight in the morning when the *Enola Gay's* crew spotted its objective. In the city below, men and women jammed the streetcars on their way to work. Giggling children scampered off to school. At precisely 8:15 A.M., the B-29 dropped its bomb. Seven hundred yards above Hiroshima, the bomb exploded like a huge flashbulb. The

A bomb of the "Little Boy" type dropped over Hiroshima

The explosion over Hiroshima on August 6, 1945

work of the Manhattan Project was complete.
But the world was never to be the same again.

More than seventy thousand Hiroshima
residents were killed in the bomb's blast. Many
were instantly incinerated by the fireball, and
their shadows lingered for years as ghostly

*It is almost impossible to imagine the devastation and human suffering
caused by the dropping of atomic bombs on Hiroshima and Nagasaki.*

silhouettes on the sidewalk. Three days later, a second atomic bomb was dropped on Nagasaki, killing forty thousand more people. And, in the days, months, and years to come, the death toll in the two cities continued to climb. The bombs released poisonous radiation that caused leukemia and a host of other diseases. Not even the Manhattan Project scientists had foreseen that their creation would have such deadly, long-lasting effects. Even today, Hiroshima and Nagasaki residents are dying of sicknesses caused by radiation from the 1945 explosions.

A tiny survivor of Nagasaki

Even the suburbs of Nagasaki were affected by the atomic blast.

On August 14, 1945, in a ceremony aboard the battleship USS Missouri *in Tokyo Bay, Japanese officials signed the formal surrender ending World War II.*

On August 14, 1945, just five days after the Nagasaki blast, Japan agreed to American terms of surrender. The atomic bombs manufactured by the crash program called the Manhattan Project had helped to end World War II.

However, the bombs also ushered the world into a frightening nuclear age. Since Hiroshima, millions of people have pondered whether nuclear weapons will someday spell the end of life on our planet. That question was first raised on the New Mexico desert in 1945. One of the Manhattan Project scientists, awestruck by the power of the first nuclear explosion, remarked, "I am sure that at the end of the world—in the last millisecond of the world's existence—the last man will see something very similar to what we have seen today."

President Truman reads the Japanese surrender to his cabinet.

INDEX

PHOTO CREDITS

Cover, Los Alamos National Laboratory; 1, Argonne National Laboratory; 2, © Buddy Mays/Travel Stock; 3, Los Alamos National Laboratory; 4 (top), The Bettmann Archive; 4 (bottom), 5 (bottom), AP/Wide World; 5 (top), Los Alamos National Laboratory; 6, UPI/Bettmann; 8, Stock Montage; 9, 10 (left), AP/Wide World; 10 (right), Stock Montage; 11, 12, AP/Wide World; 13, UPI/Bettmann; 14, 15, 16, Argonne National Laboratory; 18, UPI/Bettmann; 19, Los Alamos National Laboratory; 20, AP/Wide World; 21 (top), UPI/Bettmann; 21 (bottom), 22, Los Alamos National Laboratory; 23, 24, AP/Wide World; 25 (top), Stock Montage; 25 (bottom), The Bettmann Archive; 26, 27, AP/Wide World; 28, 29, UPI/Bettmann; 30 (top), The Bettmann Archive; 30 (bottom), Stock Montage; 31, AP/Wide World

Picture Identifications:
Cover: The mushroom cloud formed by the explosion of the world's first atomic bomb on July 16, 1945
Page 1: Technicians at the University of Chicago assembling the first nuclear reactor
Page 2: The desert near Alamogordo, New Mexico

Project Editor: Shari Joffe
Designer: Karen Yops
Photo Research: Jan Izzo
Cornerstones of Freedom Logo: David Cunningham

ABOUT THE AUTHOR

R. Conrad Stein was born and grew up in Chicago. After serving in the U.S. Marine Corps, he attended the University of Illinois, where he earned a B.A. in history. He later studied in Mexico, where he received an advanced degree in fine arts.

Reading history is Mr. Stein's hobby. He tries to bring the excitement of history to his work. He has published many history books aimed at young readers. Mr. Stein lives in Chicago with his wife and their daughter, Janna.